MIK

SUP

AND THE PHARAOH'S TREASURE

Illustrations by Rob Lee
and Ian Henderson

Muller

The desert of Egypt. A blanket of sand stretches to the horizon, interrupted only by a gust of wind or a clump of rough grass. Beneath this ocean of sand lie the ancient tombs of the Pharaohs, packed full with the treasures of an ancient civilization.

A young archaeologist is brushing the sand away from the entrance to a secret chamber . . . unaware that someone has been there before her.

Far away, a space station floats peacefully through the heavens. This is the home of a very special teddy bear and his extraordinary friend from the planet Spot. There is no gravity in space, so Spottyman and SuperTed have to wear magnetic boots to stop them floating into the air.

Suddenly, the silence of space was broken by the piercing sound of the space station's alarm.

"Bubbling blancmange!" said SuperTed.

"Great Moons of Spot!" shouted Spottyman, and, from opposite ends of the space station, they rushed towards the video monitor.

They ran so fast through the narrow corridors that they almost collided! "Get down from the ceiling, Spotty! You're making me dizzy!"

When they turned on the video monitor, an elderly woman's face appeared on the screen.

"Ah, SuperTed, I hope you don't mind my asking your help. One of our expedition party is missing. She went off to look for the City of the Dead and hasn't come back. I'm afraid she might be trapped somewhere!"

"Pulsating prunes! We'd better get there quickly, Spotty," said SuperTed, but as they turned to go, the woman shouted after them:

"Do be careful! There's a curse on anyone who enters the Pharaoh's tombs!"

"A curse! Oh, Help!" cried Spotty, who was beginning to get a little frightened. "Just the thought of a curse makes my spots ache."

SuperTed tried to reassure him. "Don't be afraid, Spotty. It's only superstition. Come on, I'll say my magic word," and in a fraction of a second he changed into his special, magic form. Spotty strapped on his rocket pack, and they dashed towards the airlock.

"What's a superstition, SuperTed?" asked Spotty as they flew towards the Earth.

"I'm not sure, Spotty, but I think it might be dangerous!"

INTRO

Meanwhile, beneath the sands of the desert, the young archaeologist made her way through the tomb of an ancient Pharaoh. Suddenly, an eerie voice made her stop in her tracks.

"Keep your mouth shut, lady, and get down those steps!"

It was Texas Pete. Together with Bulk and Skeleton, he had crept into the tombs to steal their treasures, and he did not want anyone to know he was there.

As the villains led the girl past the mummies of the Pharaoh's court, she spotted something on the wall, and shivered with fear.

"Frightened of us, are you?" laughed Texas Pete.

"No, not of you," said the girl. "It's the hieroglyph. The picture writing. It says: "Death Comes To All Who Enter Here."

Tex was not in the least worried. "A curse, eh?" he laughed. "I can see I'm going to like it here."

Skeleton was more worried. He didn't like the look of the huge mummies with their cold, blank faces. Who could tell how long they had been there and what was inside?

"Can't we go back, Tex. It's so scary here. It's much cosier outside."

"No, you can't," said Tex, and he walked over to one of the mummies and levered it open. There was nothing inside. Then he took the girl by the arm, pushed her into the darkness, and closed the door firmly. "That's what happens to snoopers!" he said, and he turned towards Bulk and Skeleton. "Now hurry up and look for the entrance to the treasure room before anyone else comes snooping."

By this time, SuperTed and Spottyman were flying over the desert, looking for the lost girl. They had been looking for quite a time and had not seen anything.

"We'll never find her in all this sand, Spotty."

"We can't just give up, SuperTed," said Spotty. "Think of that poor, lost girl."

As they flew over the dunes, they caught sight of a speck on the horizon. It was the girl's landrover. Close to it, half buried in the sand, they found a small brush.

"Let's dig here, Spotty. You never know, we might find the doorway to the tombs." Soon they swept the sand off a large, stone slab. They had found the entrance.

Inside the tomb, Bulk was struggling with a mummy.

"Cor, Tex! This one's heavy." He pulled harder and harder, trying to pull the mummy away from the wall. Eventually it began to shift.

"Oh no, I can't hold it!" he shouted, and the mummy toppled forward, pinning him to the ground.

It had been covering a doorway which led to the treasure room of the Pharaohs. There, in the centre of the room, stood a statue of Anubis, the guardian of the tomb.

Skeleton stared at the statue of the dog with horror. "I'm sorry, Tex. I've got to go. I'm allergic to dogs."

"You crazy bonehead! It's not real; it's made of gold!"

As Tex turned to admire his treasure, he heard a noise behind him. SuperTed had arrived.

Thousands of years before, the ancient Egyptians had set booby traps in an attempt to stop thieves from plundering their treasure. When SuperTed and Spottyman raced into the treasure room they stepped on a loose slab which gave way beneath them, and sent them plunging down a deep shaft. SuperTed grasped hold of a ledge, and for a few dangerous moments, both he and Spotty swung, suspended over some sharp spikes.

"Quick!" said Tex. "Let's find somewhere to hide!" The villains ran into the other room, and, finding a pile of old bandages, carefully disguised themselves as mummies.

"They'll never find us in here," laughed Tex, as they climbed into the mummies.

SuperTed and Spottyman were not far behind them. With a blast of their rocket boots they shot out of the shaft and sped into the room.

Spottyman crashed straight into Skeleton. "Fancy bumping into you," he said, looking very surprised.

Meanwhile, SuperTed had caught up with Bulk. He caught hold of the end of a bandage and gave a sharp tug. "I'll help you with these bandages," he said, as Bulk spun round like a top.

Neither of them had noticed that Tex had escaped through the entrance to the tomb, shutting the door behind him. Fortunately, he didn't get very far, because his bandages had caught in the doorway.

SuperTed and Spottyman released the girl from the mummy, and they all laughed to see Texas Pete struggling with a mass of bandages.

"I think Tex needs a little time to unwind," said SuperTed.

Later, the young archaeologist thanked SuperTed and Spottyman for rescuing her. "Thanks for your help. You see, there wasn't a curse after all."

"No," said SuperTed, and he smiled. "It was just superstition."

As they stood there, smiling and talking about their adventure, it seemed as if the statue smiled with them. Spottyman patted it kindly. "Down, boy, down," he said.